THE
MAN
WITH
RED
SUSPENDERS

Poems by Philip Dacey

MILKWEED EDITIONS
Minneapolis, Minnesota

THE MAN WITH RED SUSPENDERS
Poems by Philip Dacey

89 88 87 86   5 4 3 2 1

Published by *Milkweed Editions*
an imprint of Milkweed Chronicle
Post Office Box 24303
Minneapolis, Minnesota 55424
Books may be ordered from the above address

Edited by Emilie Buchwald
Designed and Illustrated by R.W. Scholes ©1986

Library of Congress Catalog Card Number: 85-063725
ISBN: 0-915943-11-5

This publication is supported in part by grants provided by The First Bank System Foundation; the Jerome Foundation; the Metropolitan Regional Arts Council from funds appropriated by the Minnesota State legislature, and with special assistance from the McKnight Foundation; and the United Arts Fund.

ACKNOWLEDGEMENTS

Some of the poems in this book have appeared in the following periodicals and anthologies: American Poetry Review; Ball State University Forum; Been Here Once: Hotel and Cafe Poems (Dacotah Territory); Chelsea; Chowder Review; Colorado State Review; Corona; Cumberland Poetry Review; Crazy Horse; Dear Winter: Poems for the Solstice (Northwoods Press); Elkhorn Review; Esquire; Great River Review; Happy Birthday, Minneota (Westerheim Press); Inscape; The Iowa Review; Jeopardy; KRSW Newsletter (Worthington, Minnesota); Lake Street Review; Lower Stumpf Lake Review; Memphis State Review; The Menomonie Review; Mickle Street Review; Milkweed Chronicle; Minneapolis Review of Baseball; Moons and Lion Tailes; Mississippi Review; New American Poets of the 80s (Wampeter Press); The New Jersey Poetry Journal; New Letters; New Virginia Review; The Painted Bride Quarterly; Pocket Poems (Bradbury Press); Poet and Critic; Poet Lore; Poetry Northwest; The Sensuous President by "K" (New Rivers Press); Spoon River Poetry Quarterly; Sumus; urth apl; Walt Whitman: The Measure of His Song (Holy Cow! Press); Windflower Almanac of Poetry (Windflower Press).

The author wishes to thank the Corporation of Yaddo and the Ragdale Foundation for residencies, and the Minnesota State Arts Board and the McKnight Foundation in conjunction with The Loft (Minneapolis) for fellowships to help him finish this book.

for Owen

and in memory of our sister
Joan
1932–1983

NORTH BROADWAY & GRAND

for Owen, the Dancing Policeman
of St. Louis

O, when she died
he was the traffic cop
again, the ballet dancer
so gracefully

threading a city
through his hands,
only this time he was there
at the crossroads

to lead her home,
his sister, through
the deepening dark,
no light but that

of his presence,
his only uniform
the look he gave her
as every move he made

the whole rushing hour long
signalled he was
close enough to her
to die himself.

"The most difficult corner
in the city. The most
expensive equipment
couldn't manage it."

Put Dacey in. And the human
touch eased
the knot, jam, block,
and everyone got home

safe, everyone.

Also by Philip Dacey

Books

How I Escaped From the Labryinth and Other Poems (1977)
The Boy Under the Bed (1981)
Gerard Manley Hopkins Meets Walt Whitman in Heaven and Other Poems
(1982)

Chapbooks

Fives (1985)
Fish, Sweet Giraffe, the Lion, Snake, and Owl (1970)
Four Nudes (1971)
Men at Table (1979)
The Condom Poems (1979)

Anthologies

I Love You All Day/It Is That Simple (1970; Co-edited with Gerald Knoll)
Strong Measures: Contemporary American Poetry in Traditional Forms (1985;
Co-edited with David Jauss)

*The Man With Red Suspenders is set in Bembo Bookface and
printed on acid-free Mohawk Superfine Text paper.*

CONTENTS

. . . ribs in the holy desert . . .

. . . impossible tail-feathers . . .

. . . eyes set free to float . . .

. . . ribs in the holy desert . . .

THE HITCHHIKER

I am dangerous.
I could change your life.
If you are light,
I am dark.
If you are clean
I have grease
on my knapsack.
It bulges
with your desires.
I have carried them for you
long enough.
You have passed me
many times, even
in the worst weather.

Now our eyes
meet again
but this time
you do not turn away.
This time the shield
between us
might as well
not be there.
This time, I don't even
have to hold out my thumb.

You slow down,
for no reason
anyone could steer by,
for the mere feel
of the break,
your heart racing
like an engine,
a fire harnessed
under a hood
and longing
to be out of control,

as if you knew
to let me in
is to let me
take over the wheel.
After that,
it is only a matter
of a few revolutions
before you tell me
where it is you have to get out.

WALT WHITMAN'S
ANSWERING SERVICE

Who calls here,
hankering, gross, mystical, nude?

Did you expect to find me at home?
Then you do not know me.
I am never at home.
I am always on the road.
All roads lead to the telephone;
wherever you go, on or off
the road, a telephone wire
sings beside you.

I knew you would call.
Everyone does,
in his or her own way.
All the wrong numbers you dial
are meant for me,
are the attempts of your better self
to make the call
you are afraid to make.

If you would have me know who you are,
leave no name or number,
simply give to this line
the mist of your breath
and I will recognize you.

I will call you back
unless you wait by the phone
for me to call you back.
Be confident, but be warned:
my voice could be disguised
as anything, anything.

If you love me,
if you truly wish to get through to me,
you will hang up

at the sound of the tone
and dial your own number.
If the line is busy
or no one answers,
consider yourself lucky,
you can always call again.
If the line is out of order,
remember, you are the only repairman.
If the line has been disconnected,
remember, the only phone company
is yourself.

DIALING A WRONG NUMBER

You know you have dialed
the right number.
You were careful.
You did everything
you possibly could.
It is a wrong number.
The voice at the other end
is not surprised
or disturbed.
She says she gets nothing these days
but wrong numbers
and has come to need them.
You tell her everything
you meant to tell
your other party; she tells you
what she would tell the one
who never calls.
Nothing makes sense.
You stay like this,
talking on the phone,
far longer than you know.
You exchange your past
for her past, a dime
for ten pennies, and discover
you have everything
and nothing in common,
this line, this telephone,
which by now is crackling
mysteriously. You are convinced
there is someone else on the line,
listening, making sense
out of everything.
You become uneasy, even
fearful, and tell the voice
you have much to do,
a whole book
of right numbers to call.

She says talking to you
has been wonderful,
that she hates
the correct silence,
and asks for your number.
You give her,
without even trying,
a wrong one.
With any luck at all,
she'll get through to you
again and again.

WAITING FOR THE MAIL

It's hours yet,
years, probably,
but you're waiting
for the mail. You get yours
at the local p.o., in the windowed
box. The envelopes
click against the glass
as they slide in, like bolts
in a gun, you're the target.
Hit me, hit me.
Somebody, something,
a kiss, a kick,
whatever's stamped
with authority and cancelled
before you even touch it
by shadows like stylized
waves, water
you're dying to drown in.
What you want is romance
like a brown manilla envelope,
thick, a parcel *manqué,*
the hand satisfied
to have it, hefty,
rounded, like the body
of a woman you once met
in a dream of a wanted poster,
she up there with all those others
guilty of defrauding the
U.S. mails.
Hope is the thing with
a postmark, a magic circle
naming a place
you've never been
but remember well. Maybe today
your box will be full
to the point of finality;
you'll say, "This is the delivery

to end all births,"
you'll cancel your little
rented cell in the beehive
of human intercourse
and, smiling, return
everything to sender.

THE SHOPPING LIST

In the crowded aisle,
I read the list
as carefully as I can,
but it's no use,
the list says corn
and I have put peas in the basket.
I try again,
the list says bathroom tissue
but this time my hand returns
with a ball of gouda.
Nothing is what it should be.
I try to stay calm. Surely
there's an explanation.
I U-turn into the next
aisle and find women on display,
parts and whole,
frozen or fresh.
Some gesture toward me,
like whores in doorways.
I check my list.
Now every item
refers to women.
My mother is on the list,
and my sister. Others.
The list is unreliable,
it shifts like ribs
in the holy desert,
but what else can I go by?
I study the handwriting.
It is familiar, perhaps
my wife's, or my own,
or that of a third person
long absent from my life.
And now my basket
is heaped to overflowing,
heavy, I can hardly
push it. I spill cartons

and fruit struggling
to the front of the store,
then discover
there is no checkout area.
Instead the store opens
onto a vast plain.
People walk there,
as if forever,
shopping for nothing,
their grocery carts
full of everything
they need, empty.
I turn back
into the store
and demand to see
the manager.

THE NO

The condom salesman tries them on like shoes.
He'll find the size and style for you. He has
the practiced eye and hand, the sense of what

confines just so, that you can live in,
a way to breathe without the need to breathe.
He'll see it fits you like a pair of shoes

to go anywhere in, and touch nothing,
always a sole away, or skin, the fashion
nowadays for those who'd stay clean

cleaner, cleanest in the face of faces
close enough to catch. The condom salesman
looks you in the eye a thin film protects

and asks you how it feels, the size he found
to help you make your disappearance perfect
while seeming not to disappear at all.

But you've no feeling left to tell him,
or just enough to make a sign: you'll buy.
Today the going-out-of-business sale,

and he, the salesman of the means
of going out of business, smiles to turn
aside a question about price. Who can't

afford protection such as this? Sometimes,
as any schoolboy knows, you have to lose
your life to save it. And there's the beauty

of the thing itself, whatever the style,
the sleek and shining sleeve, a work of art,
finer than a shoe, and looking—this No

manufactured in accordance with
the highest standards—just like you.

THE OFFICE MANAGER LOCKING UP

In my neat office,
only the drawer
is out of place,
open.
It is a mouth
about to say something
I don't want to hear.

And now I know
it is female,
that space,
and it is not
mine. Even if I shut it,
it stays open.

It could say
help
or I hate you
or I don't need you
at all,
but whatever it said
would curve
so as not
to fit my file.

I lean across
my desk top
and shut it.
Now there is nothing here
not arranged.
Now the whole office
cries aloud,
the silence says
murder
and order
as if they were one word.

A USED CAR LOT AT NIGHT

Love has come
to the used cars.
The moon shines down
and changes their lives.
Under the sun
they were hard, flawed,
a nervous tremor
ran through the metal.
Each was separate
from each. But now
community. Now they flow
together like water,
veering away from their past
like a car avoiding
the body suddenly
before it.
Above them, the flags.
All the long day,
bright triangles
flapped in time
to the anthems of countries
men escape from by night,
crossing a border.
Now the flags, their many
colors become a single
color dreaming desire,
hang perfectly still.
The hearts of the cars
have grown large and spiritual.
For a pure blue moment
there's a special
on eternity. Love
has come down from the sky
and cooled the fever
of the cars. The miles
in the tiny windows
roll back to zero,

a spinning declaration
of possibility. The cars
shudder and die
like one body
a sexual spasm
releases.

THE SWAN

Zeus, entering my body, pushed me out.
I had to watch the while, off to the side,
or up, or down, in some indefinable
space where I'd become pure soul, as if
I'd died. But I wasn't worried. Zeus
had promised me I'd get my body back
and get it back the better for his use.
I don't know how I saw exactly: it felt
as if I saw from all directions at once
and with the very sunlight as my eyes.

I realized soon what he was after, or whom.
I had seen her, too. Don't think a swan
only fancies swans. This woman was brimming
with herself. She lay carelessly on the sand.
The garment she wore was only there enough
to make her nakedness the more pronounced.
Swan and woman, we had more in common
than not. Still, I didn't do anything.
Who would disturb perfection? Zeus would.
If only there'd been room inside my skin
for both of us, consorting host and guest,

or maybe there was and I got conned by a god,
a selfish god who hadn't learned to share.
Whichever, I was only a spectator.
Zeus knew what to do with a swan's body.
The woman was quickly aswim in white feathers.
Those were my feathers, and weren't. It was my
other self I was seeing in action,
possibility of past and future,
the present all deprivation except
for knowledge. I was rich knowing my lack.

Zeus left without a word. I contracted
to re-enter my home, happy to be back
from my nowhere, but my home had changed. It echoed

with its recent past. I was confused. I had
a memory of doing what I did not do.
The woman slept now on the sand. Her breath
lifted my feathers. I wanted to sleep, too.
I touched, with the tip of one wing, her hair.
I lived between two dreams, of being-here
and not-being here. I said a swan-prayer
as I lay down my long neck beside her:

> *My history has changed now with this act,*
> *which will test everything I do. The god,*
> *once come, is always there as ghost longing*
> *to come again, to take the place that was his*
> *before. I am no swan if I am only*
> *swan. I saw those two look eye to eye,*
> *or burn eye to eye, a conflagration*
> *marked by shudders at the view, and knew*
> *I witnessed there my invitation*
> *to a death by fire, to come and disappear,*
> *perhaps forever, into swan-desire.*

PLACATING THE GODS

They are alive and well,
opening trapdoors in beds
the moment you touch your wife,
leaving your fingerprints
on empty packages
your friends receive in the mail.
And when they are not
taking your serious words
and setting them
in cartoon balloons,
they are busy turning you
invisible as you try to address
a large audience.

So devise your own rituals:
circle your house three times
before entering,
stir with the wrong end
of the spoon,
offer yourself like a leaflet
to strangers on streetcorners.

If none of these help,
what the gods want is humility,
that for meals
you savor stones,
that a discarded thread
be a means
for stitching a life,
that when you walk you be amazed
you are not falling.

Above all,
follow this directive:
lay out each night
the small snack of yourself.
In the morning,

when you inspect the plate,
you will be gone.
Spend the day
finding yourself.
Say thank you.

THE PIANO

for Bill Holm

"O my enormous piano"
Frank O'Hara

I'll take you everywhere, piano.
I'll coddle your keys.
You'll be first in the van,
thick, quilted pads
almost making you sick,
only your rollers showing.
I'll bang on the van wall
at stops, my black
gleaming monster, you'll be
all right.
      The window in the corner,
light coursing through it like grace,
will be yours. Pick the flowers
to stand around. They'll listen;
we'll all listen.
      And the floor,
waxed to ice, will catch you up
and show you again underneath,
flat-bottomed, implausible, slick.
My totem, wait!
      We'll lock them all out,
the blasted-eared, the thick-fingered,
the pickers and rompers,
the dead.
      O my enormous piano,
I plunge my hands
deep into your heart,
your wide, stringed hollow.
I touch your sides
and come up
unbloodied.
Cool giant, help me,
I am full of blood.

THE MAN WITH RED SUSPENDERS

for David Jauss

Student: What are the limitations of fiction?
Teacher: First of all, you can't write a story about a man
       with red suspenders.

I am the man with red suspenders,
alive in this poem.
For years I wandered from short story to short story,
seeking admittance.
Men at desks, like hotel clerks,
looked up to inspect me
then quickly went back to their ledgers.
I think some were amused
and disinclined to take me seriously;
others seemed affronted
I should dress so.
Oh, I could have found a place easily
by changing clothes,
but I need these suspenders,
not the way firemen in the old joke
need them, but because without
their snap and gaiety,
I fall down.

My happiest moments
were passing in front of store windows:
there, with the fruits and jellies,
the trinkets for ladies,
the bolts of cloth stacked to the ceiling,
all the goods of the world,
I could see
my red suspenders,
two strips of fire,
two passionate
dreams,
two strokes in a child's painting
of nothing in particular.

But the winters were long and cold.
I grew desperate.
Then I saw a sign flashing on and off:
POETRY—VACANCIES.
I entered. The man at the desk
was asleep. I poked him with my finger.
He stirred and looked at me
through half-open eyes.
I told him what I wanted.
"Sure," he said, looking me over, "We take anyone."
Then, as he picked up his pen, "Even fools."
Now I have hooked my thumbs
behind my suspenders
and my chest swells:
I am as pleased as Punch
to be here.

. . . impossible tail-feathers . . .

WHAT SHE SAID

I am a full-bodied nude
lounging in a forest
on a bed of moss.
A man has placed me here
for purposes still forming
and told me not to move
unless it be to lift a hand,
like so, to a hip, or else to stir
in a general way.
                    I have seen him
move about this scene, in and out,
among the trees, arranging
the fall of my hair, studious
of what the light,
whose source is unknown,
does to me, and never
speak, never
break the illusion with a kiss.

Perhaps, before he returns,
before I resume
the pose so finely struck
between earth and sky,
the pose
so intimate, yet so distant,
you can take my hand,
this one, flushed with blood,
and touch it to your lips.
Perhaps, before he returns,
you can love me.

A DREAM OF PRESIDENTS

They have come here,
not running,

but with a movement
like floating.

They have come here from all over,
laying aside their burdens.

It is a plain.
Here they receive

the votes of the grass.
The horizon is their party.

The sun is always overhead:
the tops of their skulls burn

but here the presidents
cast no shadows.

The rhetoric of the sun
persuades them to go naked.

They lie down,
exposed.

Their bodies begin to open,
no one can see this happening

but the presidents themselves.
They begin to weep,

reaching their hands into the darkness
of each other's bodies

and drinking. They are forgetting
about numbers, the wind

is coming up
and their bodies

have begun to glow,
like embers.

HE DISCOVERS
THE WORD
"INVAGINATION"
IN THE
DICTIONARY

Invaginate me,
O God of invagination.
Fold me over
myself,
petal me back
to a bud.

I would be dark and secret.
I would have a space
I am proud of
no one sees.

CRIME

She lies at the side of the road, naked,
having been raped, beaten, tossed from a car.
You made her up. She is your soul's image.
Who are the men speeding away? You are.

THE WINTER THING

We were going to
but the storm came.
It would have been the first time
for either of us.
The place and hour were set.
Everything was ready.
The storm said no.

The storm poured out of us,
white denial,
white reticence.
We filled the road between us
with that whiteness.
No cars could move,
they wondered so
at the elaborate system
of beautiful roadblocks
people are as good
as wind at creating,
drifts this high
from shoulder to shoulder.

So we left our homes
and went out into it,
the Thing we had made
our environment, she there,
I here, and made
snow-angels, touching,
at all points,
one on top of another,
you couldn't tell them apart.

HE RESTRICTS HIMSELF TO
READING ONE POEM A DAY

for Don Olsen

This is it.
This is one woman
for a lifetime.
You have
to pick a good one.
You have to have
good instincts.
All through the day,
over and over,
that one poem,
in many different
positions,
lights.
You know there are others,
they wait with their
powerful verbs
and surprising adjectives.
Ah, the drifting perfumes
of their measured
irregularity!
Tomorrow, in another life,
your tongue may follow
their contours,
may slip in and out
of their looping vowels,
their consonantal gates,
but today you are faithful
to this one. Today
you believe you cannot exhaust
what's between the lines,
that staying on good —
that is, burning — terms
is just a matter
of paying attention
(and a little imagination),

and that the child
who repeats a word
until it's nonsense
knows the truth:
repetition can lead
to strangeness,
not familiarity.
You do this
all the while you suspect
someone else may be saying her
right now.

SOMEONE

When I asked him how he was,
he told me about money.

When I asked about his wife,
he said dollars and cents.

When I asked about his children,
he said cash register.

When I brought up the war,
he said aught aught aught aught.

When I mentioned the weather,
he said brother can you spare one.

When I told him a joke,
he put a slug on his tongue.

When I said nothing,
he held his wallet to his ear.

When I asked for a favor,
he said international cartel.

When I told him my secret,
he whispered what the moon costs.

When I asked him about money,
he said, I'm dying for love.

FAIRMOUNT PARK

(East St. Louis, Illinois)

My father always bet to show.
The other fathers bet to win.
My father kept it in.

He took me with him
to the window
so that I learned how
to put the money down
and call the number out.

He never lost a lot
and sometimes won a little.
He's growing old now in a house
as safely hedged as
"Valentine, to show."

I liked the colors
of the cards, the tickets
where the future rode,
and liked the way, the races done,
the floor was rainbowed,
a city street confetti-bright
after the heroes' parade.

And always an old woman came,
sifting the litter for a winner
mistakenly thrown away.
Why did I think
because my father bet to show,
she walked bent low?

The horses' hooves that pounded
in the stretch are now my heart
gone wild to know
my love, my fairest mount,
will soon be at the wire
and then it will be out—
if I'm my father's son or not.

WILD PITCHES

You've been holding back
long enough, Son.
Stop aiming the ball.
Let your power,
that animal,
out. Don't worry
about hurting me.
I'm in my father-squat
behind homeplate, like a frog,
the soon-to-be-a-prince frog,
nothing and nobody
can stop that story.
Not even you. The whole world
squats so, just waiting
for you to throw the ball
as if you meant it,
an angry word,
an idea
to change the world,
a declaration
of love. It's true
some pitches will go wild.
At first a lot will.
But remember,
God is somewhere
with a mask and protector
for his chest and nuts
and catches every
wild pitch there is.
He's a scrambler.
So let that arm uncurl
and snake out
like the snake that girdles
the world—whip-snake,
diamonded and poisoned
to the point where
the wildest pitch
is the one that stays
in your hand.

THE OTHER WOMAN

You let her in the door.
She goes to the ceiling.

You coax her down.
She hides behind furniture.

You offer her brandy.
She begins drinking the air.

You play records for her.
She spins away, darkly silent.

You give her a gift.
She wants only the wrapping.

You touch her shoulder.
A strange fruit blooms there.

You call her names.
She begins quoting your life.

You slap her.
She places a candle in your fist.

You tear off her clothes.
She numbers the parts of her body.

You threaten to kill her.
She grows fat and serene.

You kill her.
She gives birth to your wife.

THE NIGHTGOWN

(She to him.)

It was never a favorite of mine,
But now it is, now that it's ruined.
Ruined so well. It seems to have risen
Swinging out of reach only to linger
Close, in air, a low-cut ghost, and tempt me
With meaning. The secret of the torn nightgown.
A cheap thriller for insomniacs. Still,
If the first rip was an accident, mere
Enthusiasm of a hand, yours, Love,
The second and third, and the others past
Counting, had the color of romance,
The unfamiliar. This was something new
For you, no beast, usually, though no
Angel either. You for the Peaceable Kingdom
Of human animals. So what was I to make
Of all this willed wildness, this sacrifice
To the god of nylon, and me in it?
I heard one sound follow another. Notes?
Was it musical necessity
That called it forth, a set of deliberate
Variations on a theme of chance?
If so, the ear, the musical ear, was tuned
To the modern, the rending become a higher
Harmony, immeasure, ouch, as measure,
Touch, and touch again. Touché. Or were you
Just touched, mad, a monk, and fingering
A rosary, mock-rosary, of wounds,
Nothings, bead after bead of them, little
Absences meant to woo The Great Absence?
You wouldn't know. You were too busy filling
With these possibilities, what came in
To you looking for a home, a home to leave.
Or wouldn't know perhaps because you simply
Shrank to the white rock of your fist. I saw it,
In fishy carlight sliding through the room,

Stopping the river of my gown. Great grip,
To catch a river so! Oriental
Flow, fertile wave-scroll, enough female
Water for the whole universe to swim in.
And you had it: jammed, logged, hogged, you name it,
Bunched to dead flowers, bouquet of power.
Nevertheless, and whichever, and so be it—
There was, after all, kissing, fore and aft,
And I am not my nightgown, though I'm sheer—
That night stays and stays, a stay, a spine,
A stiff time run through me I hang on,
That hangs on me, too, my making of it.

But, meanwhile, the simple slick fact collects
Wrinkles under the bed, where I kicked it.
I suppose I could throw it out but that
Would be a lie: it's rubbed against our lives
Enough to be all static; it clings, a skin.
I'd rather use it, thread its lips shut (sh!)
And add it to the children's attic heap
Of costumes they daily gaily go in
And out of, permutating energy.
Would one of them stop to notice the scars
And wonder at the wear? Regardless, I'd
Deck play with the past—our best, most lost dress,
Its haunting lines asway from the hips down.
But not you. You imagine something as
Profoundly useless as a work of art—
Or stuffed moose's head—the tell-tale garment
On display to tease guests into questions
They don't dare ask, its black mass all arranged
To soft mountain range behind glass, a box,
Museum-piece, with one or two items,
Ring, stone, for accent, cross-texture, the whole
Clear on the wall, a plaque, but not clear at all,

Commemorative of what event in history,
What deus ex nightgown come here to tear
Time open like a toy with workings, tick.
I rehearse, to reject, your idea of
Packaging raw love like an artifact.
I'll just leave the nightgown under the bed,
Though *Good Housekeeping* wouldn't approve.
To catch dust. Or us. Or be the shadow
We cast through solid objects when we sleep.

OWNING A WIFE

Who can own a woman
with brown stars on her back?

That cool expanse exceeds
whatever the measure says.

I peer close, a convert
to the new astronomy.

At the tip of one small finger
I have all these constellations.

But really I have none.
Nor, even, does the woman:

the stars belong as water
belongs in a clenched fist.

THE DACEY PLAYERS
PRESENT
A SORT OF ELEGY
FOR G.M.H., 1844–1889

I saw my child die that day
As Father Hopkins, in a play.
On Father's Day it was, and I
A one-man audience. To die
So, rising for applause, is best.
But even so. Even so . . .
                              The last
Dishes cleared, my wife and sons duck
Behind a screen (sweet buzz of back-
Stage noises) they now whisk away
To show—a sick room? Is this gay?
A gift? What gives? There's Austin, five,
Stretched on a cot, barely alive
And got up like a priest, a long
Black cassock almost swallowing
His small body whole. "I'm too late,"
Says the doc, Florence—that's my coat!—
Then exits to come back as one
With the holy viaticum—
Or, to be exact, potato chip.
Crunch, crunch. But before soul can slip
Into heaven—Mom's got his hand—
Emmett, one of a bright angelband,
Pops up from behind our old couch,
All gauze and grins, and leans to touch
His younger brother's dying head.
Whose eyes open. Wide. Sees—God!—God
's messenger. Shock of—what?—joy? awe?
Tickle of time's destroy, love's law.
Says, in a light voice, "I am so
Happy." It's Hopkins! My (half) hero
Brought back to life by my family
To die again, thanks, just for me.
To do the death-bed scene: here doth lie

A tongue in cheek. Now *I'm* so happy
I'm clapping before the last gasp he
Doesn't recover from. Curtains.
I mean, curtain.
                    O Wife and Sons,
You did it very well, too well,
This happy death theatrical,
I did not want to see it end,
If one can wish on anyone
To die again, again, again.
It takes such practice, dying well,
A lifetime's not enough, or else
It is, and some perfect the skill
Long before they hear the call.
Our Jesuit was one like that;
Though dear, he feared he would get fat
With earth, so watched what he ate
To such a point he came to dine
On clouds, with shadow-sauce. Amen.
But you build heaven here by play
By feast for more than just our sake.
You'll understand me when I say,
Is there any more of that cake?

THE SHARD

It could have been a beach and what I held
a shell, the way I put it to my ear.
Fay, all of four, said she wanted to hear.
But the beach was railroad tracks, and the shell

a shard of train, like broken pottery,
though heavy, iron, and green, as big as a fist.
These were the same tracks Fay and I crossed
night after summer night as we made our way

uptown for gum, popcorn, ice cream; a treat.
We lived the father-and-daughter dream. What
could I do then, as that fragment grew hot
in my hands, molten even, but say, *Sweet*

*Child, listen, you can hear the whistle blow
down through the long years,* and wish it were so?

NOT GOING TO SEE THE MOVIE ABOUT A NUCLEAR HOLOCAUST'S AFTERMATH

Here. In the way
I turned away from my wife
is all the horror
I need to consider.

A great white light
blinded me
and I wandered for years
in a desert.

I would tell you how
eventually
the green place
came to meet me,

but that would be a lie.
This poem
is radioactive.
I am sorry.

WALKING AMONG THE RUINS

They picked their way. Partly out of
carefulness, so as not to stumble,
or stumble again, but also out of love
for what they walked among. Not
that they loved the ruined state,
although they saw some qualities in this or that
they'd never seen before, when newness
meant a shine it was hard to get beyond.
They had lived here, that's all, and at
a time in their lives when years
were monumental, and could fall.
The peacefulness of the place struck them
hard. It was now, finally, itself,
they thought; we maintained it
too well too long. A bird settled
on a pillar that was like the right word
for keeping the lid on; now it held up the sky
and the bird thought that was something to sing about.
They had brought their lunch. Why not?
They would make a picnic of the past,
or try to. Would sit among these toppled
forms, that were themselves in another
life, and spread a little feast
until you couldn't tell the difference
between the present and the past.
Feeding themselves on what
they remembered, on what they made
of what they remembered, they'd notice
how the shadow kept its distance so badly
from what it loved and, noticing,
begin to appreciate the new
aesthetic, a sense of design courtesy
of gravity.
                    If they were still,
or still enough, animals would come,
small, dumb creatures to be intermediaries
between the ruins and these lovers

of the ruins, these caretakers,
by crawling the ruins into motion,
crawling over each other as well.
Lizards, first one or two, then,
like luxuriant growth, fans of them,
turning the stones to sleepers
awakening from a dream
and heaving, stretching, with desire.

ROCK

1. Picking Rock

for Joe and Marcella Matthys

Renters pick fast and loose;
if you own the land, you pick close.

You can pick a field clean one year,
come back the next, and find more.

They rise up from somewhere far below.
Just how far, I don't know.

It's a rain,
but slow, and upside down.

The higher up you get,
like this tractor seat,
the easier they are to spot.

Sometimes I think there are
pregnant ones down there.

Most are granite, some are limestone.
This is no work for one person alone.

There's one kind, blue-black,
that's twice as heavy as it looks.

This one looks like a brain.
Somebody was thinking too hard again.

Here's an old Indian hammerhead.
You can see where the leather strap fitted.

Sometimes it seems everywhere you look
there's a rock.

2. Anniversary Poem

Eighteen years,
the rock anniversary.
Not precious stone, that rock,
but rock we pick

at Matthys' farm. Clearing
the field. We've picked
this field before, and will
pick it again.

The rocks are never done
rising. We bend over more
than we stand up straight.
For harvest, hard things

we pile up, bread,
little loaves, on a plate.
The exercise is good.
We sleep late.

Rocks rise in dreams.
Keep rising. Lift themselves
to heaven. This time
we hold on for the ride.

BOURGEOIS POEM

This is not the bourgeois poem
you think it is. The father
is not a father
but the dictator of a small
Latin American country,
nor the mother a mother
but the peasantry the dictator
abuses. The children
are the land itself,
innocent, seasonal,
trampled upon
by the boots of the dictator's men,
watered
by the tears of the peasantry.
When milk spills
at the breakfast table,
blood runs
in the streets of that country.
When a door slams upstairs
between two faces,
men in suits and uniforms push away
from the opposite sides
of a long polished table and say
it is no use.

Right now someone
seems to be kissing
someone else in the poem,
but actually a young man
on a dusty road in that country,
coming upon his enemy,
has experienced a strange impulse
of good will. Something about the light,
perhaps, it is evening,
or the frayed shoes of the other.
The young man shoots, of course,
the impulse gets lost

in the habit of killing,
but not entirely, a colorful
bird, flushed by the shot,
rises from the nearby forest,
hovers, as if thinking
or being thought, then flies off,
trailing his impossible
tail-feathers. He looks like
the rainbow
a ray of light through a leaded-glass
window becomes
on a living-room floor.

. . . eyes set free to float . . .

THE RULES

"Women is not allow in you room; if you burn you bed
you going out; only on Sunday you can sleep all day."

Sign in Pioneer Inn, Maui, Hawaii

Keep you trouble to youself.
We no want more than that
We got. We call police if
You money is hot.

If you lonely, go on street
Make good time.
No sit in room for weep
And call her name.

If feel good, keep down
You singing. We got all
Work to do, no time
For happy fooling.

You pay before you sleep.
You no sleep, we keep
You money. If
Don't you like, is tough.

When hot go cold
The water, blow on it
Or do without. Be glad
You got what you got.

Follow rules
Or we go bust you head.
In room no sales
And keep you shoes off bed.

THE NEW LOVE POEM

The new love poem
is known for its honesty.
The new love poem says
I don't love you.

The new love poem
remembers the old love poem
in which a woman's body
was compared to the entire world.
The new love poem tries not to feel
superior to the old love poem.

The new love poem can live
on a steady diet
of bitter fruit. The new love poem
thinks sweets
are for children.

When the new love poem sleeps,
it dreams
of getting old,
of shrivelling to a chrysalis,
of something with wings
and color so loud it talks
emerging
to thrill someone who doesn't know any better
and who doesn't want to.

PAC-MAN

Sometimes the best move is not to,
is to wait and see how the ghosts
are behaving. They'll flutter away
if you pick the right place to be still

and you can clear one entire
side of your life before they return.
They will. They always do. The deadly
butterflies. The delicious

deadly butterflies: you have a mouth
like a wedge of pie that's missing
and you come from the Japanese word
for eat. Paku, paku. And

sayonara. The power pill
in each corner, swallowed,
gives you a chance at the ghosts:
you'd swear to watch them run

they didn't regenerate each time
at the reincarnation center.
But be quick: electricity
is just lightning pretending

to be permanent. Soon
the balance of power shifts again
and the open mouth of the devourer
issues a silent scream: Scram!

It's then your touch on the joy-stick
matters to take you around corners
and down speedways, all the while
what's counting are the video wafers

you can call your own, one communion
after another, little lines
like hyphens connecting the parts
of a life, compounding it. Even

when you die, the total stays,
a ghost itself whose only imperative
is haunt, which means eat
or be eaten, which means

a strange music as a sign
transformation is taking place,
which means eyes set free
to float, and see.

HAMLET REVEALED

It wasn't Claudius who did it,
bent over the king's ear so fatally,
it was Gertrude, though it wasn't liquid poison
she poured in the bell of that ear,
it was words, that went straight to his heart
and killed him, though not right away. The play
was wrong on that, too, condensing most of a life
into minutes. He walked about for years
while the words did posset and curd the blood
and the bark that formed all over his smooth
body was just a thought of his that came
between himself and his entire kingdom,
inside and out. The thought was child of the words.
No wonder Hamlet was indecisive,
mere hebona would have been a simple case
of murder, but words—he knew as well as
his mother about sticks and stones and words.
Oh, those latter hurt, all right, but only
if you let them. And the father—anybody
who goes to sleep in his garden after lunch
is asking for trouble. Your defenses are down.
It's a miracle he made it to king.
His shrink, whom Shakespeare revised out in later
drafts, was of the opinion it was suicide, fear
of power. Like son, like father. Which two
shared a love of purity. That's why Gertrude
liked Claudius, the old goat. And that's why
Ophelia went mad. It's a good thing Hamlet
died at the end: he'd have been too nervous
under the crown to prove "most royal,"
as Fortinbras claimed. Try royal pain.
Claudius and Gertrude were actually the most sane,
they knew how to have a good time. No
regrets, in smooth blank verse, was their motto.
Power, love, a little dirt on the hands,
and if someone called them a name, why, they'd kiss
instead of listen. They wouldn't read this.

HOPKINS TO WHITMAN:
FROM THE LOST CORRESPONDENCE

"I always knew in my heart Walt Whitman's mind to
be more like my own than any other man's living."

—GMH, 1882

So at ease, so American, so at home in the world
In that portrait you look out from. At me?
You say so. "I am with you. I am as good
As looking at you." I would like
To believe you. Would like to think that pose
Is addressed to me, the collar unbuttoned,
The hand on the hip (the other democratically deep
In a pocket), and the soft hat tilted carelessly
O so carefully that I, looking and wondering, might hear,
"Comrade."
                    Comrade. I am lonely. (You see,
I shall never send this and therefore can tell
The most outrageous lies. For I have my Christ,
My only lover, for whose sake I left behind
Your book, touching I did indeed touch a man, at Bridges'.
That's Robert. You'd like him. Athletic. Rowed for Eton.
Until last year a physician but now devotes
All his time to poetry. Destined for great things.
Like yourself, Walt.)
                    I like to say your name:
Walt. Walt. Walt. Walt. Walt.
You would have less love of mine. I do.
And less love of my garb than I feel for your
Open dress, roomy and airy, a type
Of the American land itself. I am a black-robe.
Worse. A Jesuit. I know what you say of priests.
I am your reversed image, as you are mine.
I still remember the shock when my Uncle George,
Who took up photography immediately it crossed from France,
First showed me my other self: all my shadows
Blazed white, all my sunniness gone black.
That same shock again, when I encountered you,

Though this time gradual, reviews in *The Academy, Athenaeum,*
Rosetti's edition, then everything, in Bridges' library —
The difference between Paul's conversion, at a flash
On the road to Damascus, and Austin's, sweet a-building.
You so robust, manly, a prophet of good cheer;
I but animated dust, Manley, mere. And I, too,
Write poetry. But write it in a dark corner
And leave it there. For the God of Dark Corners.
You take yours out-of-doors and it expands
Ever rarer, ancient aether, to the stars.
Your gab a gas; my words a web. And I wait.
For prey. Pray to catch Christ. Fast. To eat.
How could any two be so different?
We each must be the other's Hyde.
(Do you know Stevenson over there? The book,
No doubt too heavily shadowed for such as
You and your countrymen, has caught on here.)
I mounting a cross, you laughing at loss:
The counter-colored squares of a harlequin.

Yet. Yet. The point of the horrible fable
Is they are one. Bridges tells me someone
Wrote of you as a modern Christ. Years
In the hospitals. The sick lifted
To your breast. Not that I myself
Am fixed at any cross-point. No, my Self
Is too much indulged. I am one of your
Naked swimmers. I splash and roll.
My belly, for all its thinness, glints.
Or perhaps I am the twenty-ninth. Perhaps I am
The lady herself, behind the curtain, careful,
Indulging herself in restraint. In touching them

Nowhere, she touches them everywhere.
The sun is so hot upon the water.
I must give it up. I write to tell you
I shall not, will not, touch you anymore.
The sun is too hot upon the water.
I must kill my Hyde, lest he kill me.
He wants love, and he is not my Lord.
But how kill him, and miss my own heart?
Walt, who does not hear me now,
Help me. May your brotherly love,
Be it earth- or heaven-begot,
Enfold one hard upon his dark way.
Yours, and not,
                    Gerard M. Hopkins, S.J.

CHARIS WILSON

from "The Edward Weston Poems"

Anything could start it. That strange X.
The X by which Edward lived and by which
I came to learn to live. Fill in the value.
We'd be on a trip in one direction,
the target known, labelled, fixed and strung,
when something going the opposite direction
would stop us and turn us around. We'd
become the target then, the ones who meant
to be an eye themselves, ourselves, eyed
by the single beam of nature, chance, some
Other we'd given no thought to. Picked out
we were, and spun, until Edward's eye saw
with that Other's, reciprocal, whereupon
the lens leaped, the preying lens, I prayed,
with my body, prayed to the god of lenses,
a new god, only come down days, it seemed,
still dewy from the mountain, where he waited.

Once the sun sent a shadow down across
a window Edward meant to shoot me through.
All morning he'd fussed to make something out
of the scene's clutter of props and givens
but had for his efforts only atoms,
disjuncted worlds flying willy-nilly,
until a cloud sailed away, a farewell
that proved a greeting, and light leaned in, at
just the right angle, one that caught me square
across the face, so I became jaw, cheek,
alone, and he was freed from portraiture.
Then the clods collected, an earth appeared.
Xed not out but in. An equation lived,
we were A and B, whose meaning converged
on definition for the time it took
the X to declare itself, which was the time
the finger took in marrying two worlds,
which was no time at all, a photograph.

The three perfect shapes, he always said,
were a ship's hull, a violin, a woman's body.
Behind each, though, lived the shape of shapes,
the cross that gives to some their names on lines.
Those four arms receive from all four corners.
Currents meet there, and mix, beyond control,
but if we enter them, or they us, we
lie spread along a weapon's cross hairs,
divided for a point.
                    He wanted to teach me
picture-taking but I said no. I'd seen
his camera-toting "tide of women" come
and go, but beyond that I knew those clicks
signalled silence, a finger on lips, our X.

IN HARTFORD

Wallace walked with poetry in his head.
He walked on Prospect Avenue to work.
The prospect moved his feet and they, they moved
In time to prospects good but getting better.
The words were what he walked through, on his way
To work himself into a form of play
No one would understand who hadn't walked
Upright in a cloud of syllables
Between two points that had none but their sound.

His shoes wore thin. You could see right through them
To a page angelic in its careless
Love of curls and horns the letters languished
In his ears, the tootings of the cars She
Steered around him, though he heard and kept
Their clamor constantly in the line he walked
Straight on to prove, indeed, his drunkenness,
Dear drunkenness to sober up the stars.

And once, a widow saw him, rocking, stopped,
And back a step to take it out, the X,
Then striding on, he'd got it right, the Y,
And strides on still, our Z, the natural end
Of any A who takes his walking
Seriously enough to fly.

THE FISH IN THE ATTIC

They refuse to come down.
They refuse to say
what they are doing up there.

You go up the ladder to coax them,
you get their silent, openmouthed
stare through the trapdoor.
The secret they've always kept
they're keeping higher,
near the roof of the house.

They investigate old trunks,
their flat noses bumping the locks,
looking for letters
still wet with emotion
after all these years.

They pretend they can live there
forever, swimming, flying
to the peak of the attic
in a gesture of getting water.

At night, as you sleep,
they pass over your head,
making an untranslatable
pattern amidst
what you have discarded
or do not know you need yet.

On a cold morning,
when ice has formed on the roof,
you will find them
huddled near the beams,
strangely waiting
for a fisherman to cut the hole
they can escape through.

SKATING

Skating on the surface of my life,
I saw myself below the ice,
another me, I was moving fast
above him, he was moving slow,
though he kept up. There must have been
some warp of being twisting
us together so, two different speeds
head to head, or feet to feet, or,
better, shoulder to shoulder, brothers,
that's the way it felt, but separated
by a death, an ice, a long wall
laid down upon the world to lock us
into rooms. Knock, knock. Are you
there? He was, and waving, though
it was a distant wave, an outer-space
wave, as if he were umbilicaled
and drifting off between the stars. The stars
skated on that ice, too, and went so fast
they seemed not to move at all. Perhaps
he was the one sped swerveless home,
an arrow, while I dream-skated,
my two blades, for all their dazzle,
leaving the ice unchanged, and top was
bottom and bottom top, but who could say?
I only knew I wanted to break through.
I wanted the ice to melt to let
us sink together, two lovers in a bed,
or crack, a warning sign missed, while
the stars swam around us like fish
lit up from within by something
we could never name, nor wished to,
lest the light fade. But the ice held,
because it was wiser than I was,
because two is more than twice one,
because the air and water made a pact
to disagree while I skated on
the surface of a life I thought was mine.

SAILING

And the keel hummed. The keel made music,
guiding the ship. I'd never heard a keel
hum before. I'd never been that close
to one, above it. Someone
had turned the crank to make
the keel descend, as if from heaven,
down, down, to take its place
amidst the fluid world. We couldn't
see it, it was as if invisible.
It did its work in such a way
we couldn't watch. It could have been
a spirit. It sounded like one,
the spirit of the ship.
I remembered an old poem,
a barnacled poem, sea-stained,
which had a ship which had a spirit
and they sped, they sped.
We sped. But this spirit, keel, or hum
had two notes, high and low,
that alternated as we rocked.
Was it a lullaby? It was deep
in someone's throat. Even the high
was low. Whose? I felt it was my
voice, one I'd never used.
A self beyond the self. The sex
of the being mattered and it had no sex
though the song I heard was mate-to-mate.
And spray hung from the ropes
in the form of notes; the whole scale was there,
beckoning. I loved that keel,
that meant us well, though the ship sank,
soon enough, and all perished.

THE SAFE

The safe, in falling, struck me on the head.
I saw it coming but was mesmerized.
I knew that if I stood there I'd be dead
and voices called to urge me to the side

but the sight was so spectacular a god
descending in a blaze of light would not
have fixed me more. The safe was beautiful
and fast. The black shone like a star gone all

wrong and proud of it. Gold trim sang to me.
And the dial spun rapidly, like some core
at the beginning of time. A baby
at a breast could scarcely love its mother more

than I, looking up, loved that murderer.
Or loved what issued from it. A shower
of gold. The door swung open on the way
down. I felt I'd lose my breath from awe

or from the airless press of coin before
I'd lose it from a blow. Underwater
to a non-swimmer must be like that: pure
element, no room politely to defer.

But I swam free of that precious flood just
in time to meet the thing itself, the great
black open womb bearing down, passionate
to a fault, whereat I had the strangest

thought: that I was like a mirror inside
which something equally great, black, and wombish
was rising to meet, in an open rush,
its perfect mate. When they'd meet, I'd be dead.

They met. I died. But not before I sang
it was a privilege to die like that,
the victim of treasure, inside and out,
as the tumbling money rang and rang.

THE PAPER CLIPS

The paper clips lie clean
and neat in the swath
of moonlight through the window.

Something has come over them.
A dream of a new life.
A dream of disarray.

A dream, even, of death.
The paper clips want
to unbend and hold nothing

together, nothing back.
The silver wire sings
of the end of its song.

The papers blow away.
The sheets rise to the moon,
who loves them, with naked breast.

THE READER AT MIDNIGHT

for Pauline Chard on her 75th birthday

She reads late at night
while the others are sleeping.
It is her habit, her choice.

She has done this for years,
page after page,
to get the whole story

in lamplight, surrounded by dark,
by the sounds people make
as they fall into dreams.

The ghosts of the house gather round her,
whose hair is as white
as the page marked like years

and who's keeping this vigil
for sleepers, for stories,
for the heroes her novel invokes.

And she is the heroine here,
for a reader at midnight is central,
the world spins slowly around her:

should she nod, and she does,
a wheel tilts on its axis,
disturbing a sleeper

who struggles for balance
by dreaming of her,
this figure in lamplight,

this mother, this woman,
this reader of things.

ON STAGE

"Stanislavski once said that the most interesting thing an
actor can do onstage is to fry an egg."

Penelope Gilliatt, *The New Yorker*

Yes, I've said the same thing myself
many times. That spread of white
with the yellow plop in the middle
and then the sizzle.

Of course the experience can begin
at the edge of the frying pan, where the egg
cracks—witness especially the judicious
pressure needed for a good crack—

and extend through to the delicate
task of turning the egg,
the quick, all-limbs-akimbo somersault of
white tinged with brown, the safe landing, the sigh.

And of course we mustn't forget
the man frying the egg. His head
bent down, toward the pan,
his feet firmly planted, slightly spread.

He can be either hypnotized
by the flat crackle,
or else playful, constantly prodding
the egg, reminding it of its business.

Yes, I've said the same thing myself
many times. The high drama
at that kitchen stove
can rock a stage

and burn as if with hot grease
an audience. Eat well,
the world advises, and watches, rapt,
as you get set to do so.